SUNDERLAND THEN & NOW

IN COLOUR

JOHN BRANTINGHAM & STUART MILLER

ON BEHALF OF LIVING HISTORY NORTH EAST

The History Press

First published in 2013

The History Press
The Mill, Brimscombe Port
Stroud, Gloucestershire, GL5 2QG
www.thehistorypress.co.uk

ISBN 978 0 7524 6164 9

Typesetting and origination by The History Press
Printed in India.

CONTENTS

INTRODUCTION

All of the early photographs used in this book are drawn from the William Waples Collection which is in the care of the Freemasons Provincial Grand Lodge of Durham, to whom the authors are grateful for their help and cooperation.

William Waples was born in Boston, Lincolnshire in 1884. He was apprenticed to a draper and became a window dresser in Leeds. In that capacity he came to work in Sunderland in 1908 and joined the Sunderland Photographic Association. In 1913, he started work for Binns Department Store and worked there as advertising manager until -1953; upon the outbreak of war in 1914, he joined the Royal Flying Corps. At a later date he worked for the Army Research Council and used his heavy quarter-plate camera to make over 20,000 glass negatives of documents and designs. He was an early pioneer of aerial photography – an art form which was very much in its infancy. He was active in supporting the Lambton Boys Fellowship, Sunderland Antiquarians, the Photographic Society and St Gabriel's Church. He was also a committed Freemason from 1920. He retired in 1953 and died in 1969.

Over his lifetime he devoted himself to photographically recording all contemporary aspects of the developments and changes in Sunderland. Unlike many photographers, Waples was not interested in simply capturing the disappearing heritage. He did not regard contemporary landscapes as mundane; he took pictures of the new and changing Sunderland, of Edwardians enjoying themselves on the seafront at Seaburn and Roker, and documented, unusually, the demolition of decayed properties in the old East End of Sunderland. Waples took pride in recording the urban development on the rural outskirts of the town and he captured images of fine new buildings like the Empire, which had only recently been completed; it is possible that he might even have been there on the day that Vesta Tilley attended the laying of the foundation stone.

Streets, parks, people, trams, shops and ships all fell prey to Waples' marksmanship. Above all, Waples took many pictures of the riverside – of the bridges, the quays, the coal staithes and the harbour mouth. As well as his photographic work, he was a Freemason and he took countless pictures of Freemasonry regalia and dignitaries. He documented Mason's marks on a variety of historic buildings around the country and copied sections from books relating to Freemasonry. William Waples was certainly a very busy man!

The result of all this work by this fascinating man was the accumulation of thousands of photographs in a variety of formats. The bulk of the collection is held by the Sunderland Freemasons and copyright for those used in this book resides with them. A substantial collection is also in the possession of the Sunderland Antiquarian Society, to whom Waples donated 200 glass photographic negatives in 1952.

It is a shame that Waples is not better known. His work is not in the same category as that of such artists as the Whitby photographer Frank Sutcliffe, but it is certainly of major regional significance and has provided many beautiful images for this book, which will hopefully help to raise his profile somewhat. One very public achievement, that had a vast impact on the northern region from Tweed to Tees, was his successful negotiation with corporations for the famous 'Shop at Binns' advertisement which was prominently displayed on buses and trams for decades.

Stuart Miller and John Brantingham, 2013

ACKNOWLEDGEMENTS

The authors wish to acknowledge the help of the following people: the Freemasons Provincial Grand Lodge of Durham, for making available the Waples Collection and with whom copyright for the Waples Collection resides; Bill Hawkins, for his help and advice and establishing an initial link with the Freemasons; Sunderland Antiquarian Society members, who helped with some of the captions; Jack Curtis, who gave personal stories about many of the images during a pleasant afternoon of reminiscences, shared with colleagues Gordon Foster and Vic Oates in the Donnison classroom; Vic Oates and Ann Tumman for proof reading (once again) and Sarah Stoner of the *Sunderland Echo* for material relating to William Waples.

Sunderland Then & Now has been written on behalf of Living History North East which is a voluntary organisation that collects oral reminiscences and works with a variety of public and charitable bodies in employing that material in project activities. It is based in the Donnison School, which was once a charitable school for poor girls and has now been fully restored. The eighteenth-century building is in the midst of the historic old seaport of Sunderland.

THE OLD TOWN HALL AND BINNS

OUR JOURNEY STARTS, naturally, with the iconic buildings of Binns and the old Town Hall. The site of the Town Hall was selected only after a considerable debate and Brightwen Binyon was the successful architect, with the foundation stone being laid on 9 September 1887. It took three years and £48,000 to complete and the clock holds a special place in the hearts of many Wearsiders; every New Year, runners, perhaps not entirely sober, tried to sprint the length of Fawcett Street within the twelve chimes. In 1900, following a visit of eight councillors to Paris, Brussels and Hamburg, the council took over the tramways and began to electrify the system and extend the line. The first electric tram ran between Christ Church and Roker on 15 August 1900 and the whole existing system was electrified by February 1901. Of course, the best thing about Binns was the system of pneumatic tubes in which cylindrical containers were propelled to deliver payment and bills between departments, giving children a welcome distraction from the interminable 'Back to School' sales.

IN APRIL 1941, the Fawcett Street premises of Binns were destroyed by fire following a bombing raid, but the store was soon operating again from its motor store in Holmeside and, despite major damage, Binns rose from the ashes in 1949. From the 1950s Binns became the flagship store of the House of Fraser with the exciting new feature of a spiral staircase leading to the furniture department. The new building on the west side of Fawcett Street opened in 1953 and on the east side in 1962, with an underground subway linking both stores for shoppers to move between them easily. The new Binns was notable for its restaurants, which included the Bear Pit and the Gay Tray. The Al Fayed brothers took over the firm in 1985, and following a drop in customer numbers over the next few years the east side store was closed in April 1989. On Saturday, 30 January 1993 Binns closed its doors for the final time. Thankfully, the west side premises were taken over by Central Stores and then Wilkinsons, but locals still look back to the days of Binns with nostalgia.

FAWCETT STREET FROM THE GAS OFFICE CORNER

THIS IMAGE IS probably from around 1900, because there is no electric tram apparatus and the Athenaeum still has its pillars. On the left is a lovely example of a gas lamp with its very ornate 'gallery'. The commercial premises on the left include Binns and Vincents the organ manufacturers and on the right one can see the steps of the Sunderland Gentlemen's Club. Fawcett Street was the main thoroughfare of Victorian Sunderland and on this day the crowds have stopped to stare at the photographer – not as common a sight then as it is now. The street was laid out as part of a grid of new streets covering the former gardens of Sunniside for John Fawcett by his agent William Jamieson in 1810-14. At first it was a fashionable residential street, but its width and the fact that it formed a route from the Wearmouth Bridge to Stockton Road made it more appealing for shops, banks and public buildings than as a place to live. The legendary Binns store was founded as a draper's store by George Binns in 1811. Initially in High

Street East, the shop was moved to Villiers Street and then to High Street West in 1856, and later two houses in Fawcett Street were converted into the new store.

FROM THE START, the Town Hall was too small for its purpose and various departments had to be housed in other accommodation. Plans were drawn up for its extension in 1903, but these were never carried through and its demolition in 1971 caused considerable controversy. In fact, this was at a time when town planners and architects were prone to replace old with 'exciting new' buildings, but a more sensitive approach to the restoration and reusing of historic buildings developed from the 1970s. There was a storm of protest at the demise of the clock, and the special clock tower promised by the council in compensation was never built. When the Bridges shopping centre was built the working mechanism of the clock was put on display in a transparent case, but the bells could not be used in such a confined space so a synchronised recording of the bells of Durham Cathedral were used instead. In fact, in 1983, four of them were stolen from the Civic Centre car park. Sadly, the old clock faces had corroded beyond redemption and they were replaced with 3ft-wide replicas.

SUNDERLAND CENTRAL LIBRARY AND MUSEUM FROM THE GAS OFFICE

THERE HAD BEEN a subscription library in Sunderland from 1795 and from 1810 this housed a small subscription museum. In 1846, the museum was taken over by the Corporation, which can claim to be the first Corporation to have implemented the 1845 Museums Act. The museum was moved to the Athenaeum Building in 1840 and in 1858 it was joined by the public, or free, library, which was initially for reference purposes only and there was no public access to the shelves. In 1879, the grand new library and museum and the Winter Garden, based on the model of the Crystal Palace, were opened in Mowbray

Park. American President Ulysses Grant was in attendance at the laying of the foundation stone by Alderman Samuel Storey in 1877 and it was built to the designs of the architects J. & T. Tillman. The library and the museum were managed separately until 1906, when they were both brought together, and access to the shelves followed quite some time later in 1911. Until then an indicator board had to be consulted by prospective borrowers. The first 'open access' library in the North East opened at Hendon in 1908.

DURING THE SECOND World War, the Winter Garden was damaged by a parachute mine and was later demolished. A 1960s extension took its place, but in 2001 a Lottery-funded refurbishment of the museum created a new Winter Garden extension and improved facilities. In 2003, the museum was recognised as the most attended outside of London. The museum contains a large collection of the locally made Sunderland Lustreware pottery, with other highlights including a stuffed lion, the remains of a walrus brought back from Siberia in the 1880s, and the first Nissan car to be made in Sunderland. It also contains the only known British example of a gliding reptile, the oldest known vertebrate capable of gliding flight which was discovered in Eppleton quarry. The library moved in 1995 to the new City Library and Arts Centre on Fawcett Street (occupying part of the former Binns Department Store) allowing more space for museum exhibitions. The new City Library and Arts Centre also houses the Northern Gallery for Contemporary Art, renowned for being one of the leading forums for new artists in the North of England.

THE VICTORIA HALL
AND MEMORIAL

VICTORIA HALL WAS designed by G.G. Hoskins of Darlington and built in 1870-72. In 1906, it was much enlarged by the local architect Eltringham and by then it had acquired an awful notoriety. On 16 June 1883, there was a show provided by the travelling entertainer Alexander Fay and of the audience of 2,000 children about 1,100 were in the gallery. At the end of the show an announcement was made that children holding tickets with certain numbers would be presented with a prize upon exit and large numbers of children flooded down the winding staircase, only to be confronted with an

inward-closing door bolted in such a way as to leave a gap only wide enough for one child to pass at a time; it is believed this was to ensure orderly checking of tickets. The gap was soon jammed by the press of small bodies and 183 children aged between 3 and 14 years old died in the disaster, thought to be the worst of its kind in British history. Queen Victoria sent a message of condolence to the grieving families and donations were sent from all over Britain, totalling £5,000, which was used for the children's funerals and the memorial in Mowbray Park.

THE MEMORIAL, OF a grieving mother holding a dead child, was later moved to Bishopwearmouth Cemetery, where it gradually fell into disrepair and became the victim of vandalism. In 2002, the marble statue was restored at a cost of £63,000 and moved back to Mowbray Park with a protective canopy. Newspaper reports at the time of the tragedy had triggered a mood of national outrage and the resulting inquiry recommended that public venues be fitted with a minimum number of outward-opening emergency exits, which led to the invention of 'push bar' emergency doors; this law still remains in full force today. The little gravestones of some of these children can be seen in Fulwell Cemetery. The Hall was bought by the Corporation in 1903 and modernised, but it was destroyed by an enemy landmine in April 1941.

WINTER GARDEN
AND MOWBRAY PARK

MOWBRAY PARK IS one of the oldest municipal parks in North East England and it came about when a health inspector recommended that a leafy area was built in the town, after Sunderland recorded the first cholera epidemic in 1831. A grant of £750 was provided by the government to buy a £2,000 plot of land from the Mowbray family for a new park and work began in the mid-1850s, incorporating a former limestone quarry set within what was known as Building Hill. It appears that spoil heaps were shaped into mounds to create distinctive paths amongst steep-sided hummocks and the effect was to afford the Victorian user plenty of opportunity to perambulate within a relatively small green area. The park was opened by John Candlish, Mayor and MP of Sunderland, on 21 May 1857 in

response to a demand for more open spaces in the town. An extension to Mowbray Park to include a lake and a terrace, from the railway cutting to Borough Road, was opened on 11 July 1866, and in 1879 the Winter Garden, museum and art gallery were added along the Borough Road side.

THE SECOND WORLD WAR had a serious impact on the park and it was hit with numerous German bombs. The iron structures – most notably the Winter Garden, a cast-iron bridge and the bandstand – were taken away to be melted down for weapons, and the open spaces were converted into vegetable patches. Following the war, the park fell into neglect. The Civic Centre was built on the west portion of the park and the area became known for anti-social and abusive behaviour, and was considered generally unsafe. Following a public campaign, work began in 1994 on restoring the park to its Victorian glory, funded by a £3.3 million grant from the Heritage Lottery Fund. The Sunderland Museum and Winter Garden were rebuilt, the lake was restored, the bandstand was rebuilt, and the park was re-shaped and adorned with new artworks. A large adventure play area for children was built to an 'Alice Through The Looking Glass Theme', featuring a distorted, giant chequerboard and giant chess pieces. The park officially reopened in 2000 and in the first year the park received over 800,000 visitors, making it the most visited attraction outside of London.

THE SOUTH END OF TOWARD ROAD FROM MOWBRAY PARK

TOWARD ROAD MAY have been named after Peggy Toward, who was reputed to have a public house around Borough Road and may once have been called Peggy Toward's Lonnin. The onus is on disbelievers to come up with an alternative! The buildings shown below are the Masonic temple and a chapel; the temple was built by St John's Lodge of Sunderland, which had met in fourteen different hotels and two other Masonic halls between 1806 and 1870. In 1869, they laid the foundation stone with full Masonic ceremony, moving in a year later. To the right is the old mineral line to the docks. Further down to the left was the

Victoria Hall. It was at Victoria Hall on 8 January 1872 that the first 'moving picture' show in Sunderland was given, and the Tussaud Exhibition provided the first glimpse of the new 'animated photographs' on 4 May 1896. The show included, apparently, *An Operation in a Dentist's Chair, Blacksmiths at Work in a Forge, Ejection of a Disorderly Person from a Public House* and *An American Lynching Scene.* Fortunately for decorum, the programme of the Victoria Hall also included a 'Ladies' Band'.

THE FAÇADE OF the Masonic hall is at Beamish North of England Open Air Museum and is a typical example of the type of hall built in the late 1800s. This was used by Freemasons until the 1930s, when a larger building was required and they sold the old one to the Durham Institute for the Deaf and Dumb. It was used later by the adjoining church, but by the 1970s it had been abandoned. In 1988, Beamish and the masonic province of Durham discussed where they might find a suitable building and at this meeting it was suggested that they walk around the corner to see the old hall, which they did, only to find that the building was in the process of being demolished to make way for a development of modern flats. Then began several years of fundraising to find £1.2 million to rebuild the hall, with part of the funding coming from the Masons themselves and partly from ERDF grants, and the rebuild was completed in April 2006. The museum had rescued the frontage of the hall but as that was all that remained intact, the rest of the building is a modern construction.

THE ATHENAEUM
BUILDING ON
FAWCETT STREET

WE CAN SEE in the picture below three very modern girls sailing by with their modish lace blouses and leg-of-mutton sleeves. Women's costume helps very much with the dating of photographs and this one must have been taken in the 1890s. The Athenaeum was opened in 1841 by the Literary and Philosophical Society, which was formed in 1834 following a meeting chaired by local dignitary, Dr William Reid Clanny. The new building, which cost £4,500, was designed by William Billinton of Wakefield in a Classical style with four very large stone columns at the front. It housed a museum which

was opened to the public in 1843. In 1846, the upkeep was taken over by Sunderland Corporation and the town can, therefore, claim to have the oldest municipal museum in the country. In 1858, a free library was opened in The Athenaeum. Although initially the books were for reference only, lending was introduced in 1866. In 1860, following mounting debts, the Literary and Philosophical Society collapsed and its books and museum collection were donated to the town. In January 1874, The Athenaeum became home to the Sunderland and North Durham Liberal Club, which had been commenced by Sir Hedworth Williamson.

BY 1879 THE books and museum artefacts had increased considerably and a new library and museum was built by the Corporation in Mowbray Park in order to house these. The opening of this museum brought a decline in the use of The Athenaeum and, consequently, some of its rooms were closed off. This was the beginning of the end. The Athenaeum was on a prime site for development and in 1899 the building was closed and quickly demolished, to be replaced in 1900 with ground-floor shops and first-floor offices. The nearby Town Hall was by then inadequate accommodation for all of the departments of the Local Authority and so the Borough Engineers moved in to the first floor of the new building, where they remained until the new Civic Centre opened in 1971. For a time the rear area upstairs was occupied, rather incongruously, by Burrow & Watt's Snooker Hall, proving very convenient for engineers at lunchtime! The ground-floor corner shop was renovated and for many years used as showrooms and offices for the North Eastern Electricity Board. Today the corner premises are used as offices by Gentoo – no snooker though!

RAILWAY STREET, OR BACK FAWCETT STREET

SHOWN HERE IS the town's last horse cab in the 1930s. It looks like a brougham (pronounced 'broom' or 'brohm') which was a light, four-wheeled horse-drawn carriage with seating for two passengers. The term 'cab' is derived from another common horse-drawn vehicle called a cabriolet. The brougham was either invented for Scottish jurist Lord Brougham or simply made fashionable by his example and it had an enclosed body with two doors, like the rear section of a coach. Unlike a coach, the carriage had a glazed front window, so that the occupants could see forward, and the front wheels were capable of turning sharply. The delivery vans behind the horse cab have the name Binns on them but cannot clearly be seen because one door is open. Advertisements for the store appeared on the outside of trams from March 1921, when William Waples, the advertising manager for Binns, reached an agreement with the Corporation which resulted in the slogan 'Shop at Binns' being carried on the ends of the balcony trams. Later on, Binns advertised on buses and the slogan was omnipresent throughout the North East region. The schoolboy with the school cap on seems to be in a desperate hurry.

THERE IS STILL a taxi kiosk, but it is a featureless metal hut now. William Bell, the architect of the NER from 1877 to 1922, designed the station, which was built in 1879. The eventual design arose from denunciation by the local press of an earlier 'contemptible' scheme which would not match the status of the town. It is not uncommon for the *Sunderland Echo* to campaign on behalf of an 'outraged' public. Indeed, a visitor to the town in 1879 remarked acidly: 'The much talked of Railway Station is all underground, and although well adapted to the purpose, is awfully dismal.' Sunderland must be the only city in England where the main route by car to the railway station is along a back lane. The impact of the one-way traffic system on Sunderland's economy is a constant and controversial issue, but in truth it is just one of many factors contributing to the commercial decline of Fawcett Street from its heyday, when it thronged with people in the evening and attracted trade from County Durham and South Tyneside.

THE SOUTH END OF JOHN STREET

THIS PICTURE WAS taken around 1900 and the women are wearing leg-of-mutton sleeves. The decorations could be for the accession of Edward VII, or the Relief of Mafeking, or possibly for the end of the Boer War. John Street is a street of two halves,

with the south end less commercial and more professional – the former grand houses of the middle classes being used primarily as offices. The buildings were erected between 1800 and 1850, and originally housed many important Wearside businessmen and their families. It was part of a group of residential streets that included Fawcett Street, Foyle Street and Frederick Street. Fawcett Street was named after John Fawcett, the one-time Recorder of Durham, and the other streets were named after his sons. In its early days, John Street was the epitome of sedate, middle-class respectability, a street of crinolines, carriages, maids and menservants cut off from the rowdy dockland area of lower High Street. The first invaders of residential John Street were solicitors, some of whose names can still be seen on the door plaques today. These houses were bought when the popularity of the east end of the town began to wane.

THE SOUTH BLOCK also boasted the magnificent building of the Sunderland & South Shields Water Company on the corner of Borough Road. This property has now been renovated and has become an aparthotel, known today as Hawksley House (after the great engineer Thomas Hawksley). The Water Company offices were designed by the ubiquitous Milburns, who were among the leading architects of Sunderland from the late 1880s to the early 1930s. In Bishopwearmouth they designed the Empire Theatre, the fire station and the magistrates' court, and the village centre has been described as 'Milburnopolis'. They were also responsible for the General Hospital, Bede School (now City College), the Little Sisters of the Poor Home, the Childrens' Hospital, Langham Tower, Burn Park Methodist Church and many housing estates, including High Barnes.

MACKIE'S CORNER FROM HIGH STREET WEST

THE OFFICIAL NAME of the domed building block is Hutchinson's Buildings, named after the owner. However, the occupier was hatter Robert Mackie, a silk hat manufacturer of the early nineteenth century. In those days, the production of hats involved using dangerous mercury and it is hoped that Mackie wasn't 'as mad as a hatter'! The adverts for his hats can be found in the *Sunderland Herald* stating that 'Early inspection is invited' since 'A GREAT SAVING is gained by Parties buying their hats from the manufacturer'. Soon after Robert Mackie's death, the premises changed to a draper's shops, which originally began in High Street East but moved to the corner of Fawcett Street and High Street West in the 1880s. It claimed to be the pre-eminent shopping centre of the North, famed for its selection of ladies' clothing and the latest fashions. It

also had a workshop attached which made dresses for women all over the north of England and claimed that 'the grandeur of these premises and the business purpose to which they are put is really an education to all visitors'. Oddly enough its advert refers to the 'Shopping Centre of the City'. The building pictured opposite is Havelock House.

HUTCHINSON'S BUILDINGS STILL occupy one of Sunderland's most prominent corner sites. The ground floor was constructed from cast-iron posts and stanchions erected by timber merchant and shipbuilder, Ralph Hutchinson, but these are now obscured by plate glass. The building was the focal point of the town's commercial district and a statement of prosperity. The architect, George A. Middlemiss (1815-1887), was a semi-professional figure who combined his architectural practice with an auction business. The building was much admired when it was completed and in an act of self-promotion that seems to have been characteristic of Middlemiss, he had his name inscribed on the entablature. Before 1925, the tailor's shop of F. Walker & Co. occupied the Mackie's Corner premises – 'the right shop in the right place'! They specialised in all types of gents' clothing, especially workmen's dungarees, and before the First World War they also sold football strips for local league teams. At a later date it became synonymous with Mansfield's the shoe shop, who were there for a long time before moving up High Street West. On the opposite corner from 1925, when it was rebuilt, was Walker's the Jewellers – in Walker's Buildings of course!

MACKIE'S CORNER AND THE HAVELOCK BUILDING FROM HIGH STREET WEST

FROM 1879, THE Sunderland Tramways Company was running horse-drawn trams – primitive vehicles lit by smoking oil lamps and with floors covered with straw in winter – from Roker via Fawcett Street, Christ Church, Gray Road and Tatham Street and back, under lease from the Sunderland Corporation. Other lines were added in the latter part of the century, but predominantly served middle-class areas. The first electric tram ran between Christ Church and Roker on 15 August 1900 and the system was extended to create a circular route via Hylton Road, Chester Road and Kayll Road, and to link up to Grangetown, Sea Lane and Villette Road. Then in 1903 a new line was added from Roker Avenue to Fulwell and in 1904 a branch to the Docks via Hudson Road. The Corporation electric tram system was cheap; from 1900 to 1948 passengers could travel to any part of the system for 1d (or 4p for those readers who have forgotten the days of proper money).

THE HAVELOCK THEATRE, purpose-built as a cinema, was opened in 1915 on the site of the Havelock House, which was destroyed by fire in 1898. Silent films were accompanied by a ten-piece orchestra. It had the distinction of being the first cinema in Sunderland to be equipped for sound and the *Singing Fool* starring Al Jolson was the first 'talkie' to be seen in Sunderland. It was shown between 15 July and 20 August 1929, and is always associated with the catchphrase 'You ain't heard nothing yet!' An amazing 120,000 people saw the film. It was a very fine cinema holding 1,750 people in the circle and stalls, and staffed for many years by an all-male workforce including pageboys in their blue uniforms and pill-box hats. The last film shown there was *The Three Hundred Spartans*. The orchestra which accompanied the films was replaced by a Wurlitzer organ in 1926. The cinema was renamed the Gaumont in 1960 and finally closed down in 1963.

THE HAVELOCK BUILDING FIRE

NOT UNTIL 1855 did the council decide to establish a Fire
Extinguishing Department and on 6 December of that year, the
Sunderland Fire Brigade was formed as part of the police. The Fire
Insurance Offices paid for the extinguishing of the fires and the men
were only paid when they practiced, which was the only cost of the
brigade. Records leading to the end of the century show that the
fire-fighting apparatus was not improved upon and personnel were
not given adequate training even though the town and its buildings
had grown, thus it was inevitable that a disaster occurred. The Great
Fire started in Havelock House on 18 July 1898, destroying forty-eight
businesses, twelve of which were in High Street West, eleven in
Fawcett Street, twenty-two shops and offices in John Street and three
shops in Bridge Street. Amongst the premises destroyed were those of
J. Risdon & Son, owned by Norman Risdon, which were later rebuilt in
John Street following the fire. Risdon's sold just about everything for
babies, from shawls to top quality prams, and served Wearsiders up
until its closure in 1977.

IN THE BACKGROUND on the left, thankfully untouched by the fire, is the famous Elephant Tea House building. Sunderland's townscape never achieved an architectural uniformity like Newcastle and instead offers the diverse array of banks and shops on Fawcett Street, culminating in the Venetian Gothic style Elephant Tea Rooms (1877), a building that strikes a discordant note in terms of both style and colour. The patron was an eccentric grocer named Ronald Grimshaw, who established a small empire of retail outlets in the town. Designed by Sunderland's own 'rogue architect' Frank Caws (1846-1905), the building looks like the collision of an Italian Gothic palazzo and a Hindu temple. The roofline is broken into a series of sharp gables punctuated by chimneys and, nestled between them, are niches with Indian elephants rearing their trunks beneath arches. Caws described the style as 'Hindoo-Gothic'. The elephants carry tea chests on their backs, indicating that the building was an emporium for beverages and spices from the Orient. The Venetian Gothic style became popular in Britain after art critic John Ruskin celebrated it in his influential book *The Stones of Venice* (1851-3).

BLACKETT'S
DEPARTMENT STORE

BLACKETT'S STORE WAS established in Sunderland as early as 1829 by William Blackett and it is pictured on the right prior to the Second World War. Blackett's stood at the complex intersection of Union Street, Green Street, High Street West and Pann Lane. Beyond the cupola there was a roof-garden café. The north end of the railway station and its associated taxi rank are just off the picture on the left. The store's windows were lit from the outside by electric light and there was a fine brass lift in the centre of the store, which sold everything one can imagine. One of their most famous features was the kiosks with headphones, where it was possible to hear the music before making your purchase. Perhaps not so well recalled is that they had a club system, which allowed members to buy 'on tick' with club men travelling around the colliery districts selling goods from the store. Customers came to the shop to pay their club money on a Saturday.

BLACKETT'S, LIKE BINNS, had a mechanical system which delivered bills, payments, change and receipts between customers, staff and the finance department. Binns had a system that used air pressure to propel capsules around the store, but Blackett's used the cash ball system, also designed by the firm Lamson Paragon, in which money and bills

were placed into wooden balls that unscrewed into two halves – they were then dispatched along a complex system of rails. Such internal communication systems are still in use in some stores today; indeed, it can be seen in operation at the Beamish Open Air Museum. Throughout the twentieth century there were changes to the façade of the building and also to the interior of the store as expansion took up part of Princes Street. It was damaged twice during bombing in the Second World War, but never closed for business and opened promptly at 9 a.m. every morning after the Germans did their worst. In 1963, the store became absorbed into the Hind Group, but business declined and in 1972 the store closed with a loss of approximately 150 jobs. In 1978, the premises were demolished and replaced by featureless modern shop units.

HOLMESIDE
FROM THE EAST

HOLMESIDE HAD SOME very fine and fashionable shops and around
the same time as this picture on the right was taken the best china
and glass shop, Townsend's, was located at 22 Holmeside, Wearside.
They were the sole agents for Crown Derby, Royal Worcester
and Coalport China before 1914, but stocked a comprehensive
range of products from all good suppliers. Mrs Prust's dress shop
was adjacent to Townsend's and to the right of this shop there
is a gable-end advert for Henry Tod & Son, cabinet makers and
upholsterers. The Maison Nouvelle at 4 Holmeside stocked French
and English millinery. Skerry and Bywater's specialised in court
dresses as well as evening and ball gowns, and stocked the latest
Parisian hats. Naturally, having just purchased a fine French ball
gown, the next stop would be Bolton's (5 Holmeside) to examine the
corsets. Bolton's sold a good range of lingerie and dance dresses,
and also stocked 'alpine underwear' (which probably left much to
the imagination!) Further up Holmeside was W. G. Hanning's wine
and spirit shop located opposite the former ABC cinema, where
they sold top quality champagnes, burgundies and spirits, as well as

cigars and their own pipe called (naturally) 'The Holmeside'. Later it became the well-known tobacconist's shop owned by 'Baccy' Ward.

STREET NAMES ARE an invaluable but little-studied aspect of urban development. A map from 1826 refers to Borough Road as 'back lane' (i.e. an unnamed road), but by 1844 it was named on the map, because Sunderland had since been incorporated as a borough in 1835. The name Holmeside, referring to the section between Fawcett Street and Crowtree Road, is derived from Holmeside House, a large house dating from the early eighteenth century that stood at the south-eastern end of Crowtree Lane. Between 1864 and 1876, there was a Holmeside Sports Ground on the south side of the street. Sunderland City Council's Unitary Development Plan (UDP) outlines an ambitious regeneration project for a number of sites around the city, including the Holmeside Triangle, an area adjacent to the Park Lane transport interchange, enclosed on three sides by Park Lane, Holmeside and railway tracks. Sunderland Council own 75 per cent of the land, currently occupied by a mixture of retail and commercial units including Park Lane Market. Plans for the site include the creation of extensive retail space, public meeting spaces, cafés, bars and restaurants, and a thirty-three-storey skyscraper called the Spirit of Sunderland, which would be the tallest building in North East England. The development is set to cost around £147 million.

HOLMESIDE
FROM THE WEST

THIS IS HOLMESIDE viewed from the west. It was a fashionable shopping street ranking with Fawcett Street and the imposing building on the left is 8-10 Holmeside, occupied (since 1904) by the furniture dealers Laidler Robson, who moved from Fawcett Street. They advertised themselves as 'Art Furnishers and Decorators' who had catered for 'Institutions, Mansions, Hotels etc.' and 'are pleased to undertake the Complete Decoration and Furnishing of Rooms, Houses etc. The Advantage of placing the Entire Scheme in the hands of one competent firm, cannot be overestimated, assuring as it does a perfectly harmonious *tout ensemble*, and materially minimising the cost'. For most of its life this

building has been occupied by furniture dealers; during the Second World War it was occupied by Binns and in more recent times it has been occupied by Thursby's Furnishing. There is also a sign for 'J. Piper' who was a high-class grocer and most likely had the lovely, distinctive smell of an old-fashioned grocer's. Council street cleaners can be seen sweeping the road as a tram approaches.

THE CORPORATION ELECTRIC tram system was very cheap, with fares to any part of the system just 1*d* from 1900 to 1948. On the older trams you had to sit on wooden benches and in the lower compartment they ran lengthways, often leading to uncomfortable eye contact with the passenger opposite! The downstairs compartment was reserved for non-smokers, leaving the smokers to make their way upstairs. The Corporation had a dozen single-deck tramcars that were required because they were the only cars that could pass under the bridge at Tatham Street. Some single cars were later adapted to increase passenger potential, partly because the single deck meant that smoking was not permitted and since the route was just a short one, smokers would often walk rather than ride the tram. The Corporation did not appreciate the loss of income, so adapted the vehicles to accommodate them. At a later date some of the single-deckers were rebuilt as double-deckers. Although Holmeside is still a busy street, it does not have the sort of fine quality shops which were there for much of the twentieth century.

THE OLYMPIA
EXHIBITION HALL
IN HOLMESIDE

THE OLYMPIA WAS an exhibition hall in Borough Road which opened in 1897 to mark Queen Victoria's Jubilee. The Richardson Brothers of Kelloe took over the lease in 1899 and it was transformed into a giant pleasure dome with roundabouts, gondolas, skating rink, menagerie and circus acts. Among other artists presented 'at enormous expense' was the famous Fossett family with their legendary circus. Moving pictures were introduced on the 'Olympiagraph' and Edison George's pictures of the Boer War were screened here in December 1899, all of which contributed to it being the most popular venue of entertainment in Sunderland until the early 1900s, when it fell from popularity and finally closed in 1910. It is not clear what is happening in this photograph (right), but the crowd may well have gathered for Edison George's pictures. The Olympia could not stand up to the competition of the cinema and on the site it once occupied stood one of the biggest and most luxurious cinemas in Sunderland's history, Black's Regal. It was designed by architects Gray and Evans, and built by local builders

A.J. Rankin at a cost of £100,000. It had the most modern projection equipment, staff of more than sixty, and seating for 2,550 people.

THE REGAL CINEMA opened on Easter Monday, 28 March 1932. The first full film to be shown at the Regal was *Out Of The Blue* starring Gene Garrard and Jessie Mathews. The organist was Arnold Eagle, who became known as 'Eagle of the Regal'. Black's was taken over by the Rank Organisation in 1959, when the Regal became the Odeon. It closed on 8 February 1975 for conversion to three screens and the last screening was the James Bond film, *The Man With The Golden Gun*, starring Roger Moore. It was reopened on 9 March 1975 as the Odeon Film Centre. On 28 March 1982, a special 50th anniversary concert was given by Phil Kelsall on the Compton organ and three months later, on 26 June 1982, the Odeon was closed with *One Flew Over the Cuckoo's Nest*, *Star Wars: The Empire Strikes Back* and *Mary Millington's True Blue Confessions*. The building was boarded up and abandoned for a long time, but it was to re-open as a Top Rank Bingo Club, then a Mecca Bingo Club. In July 2009, it was announced that the building and the entire block had been the subject of a compulsory purchase order.

ALBION PLACE FROM GREEN TERRACE

JUDGING BY THE dress length, the photo on the right must be pre-1914. The dominance of horse transport for intra-urban purposes is very evident; an average horse on a decent diet deposits between four and six tons of manure a year. As Bishopwearmouth grew, it sprawled along the roads around it and along the High Row (Green Terrace) and Low Row in particular, and also along the evocatively named Crowtree Lane and South Back Lane, or Vine Place. William Waples' photographs are an excellent record of the changing outer areas of the town as well as the town centre. So many photographers tend to avoid the mundane and everyday scenes, but Waples was very active in recording a living town in all its aspects. Although they do not feature in this collection, he also took pictures of housing being demolished in the old East End in the 1930s and 1940s, another unusual thing to do, but of great value to the historian.

ON THE RIGHT is part of the façade of the Priestman Building of the Sunderland Technical College. In 1939, the industrialist Sir John Priestman opened the Priestman Library with room for 10,000 books and it was full almost immediately, so that the problem with lack of space continued! The building was also home to the Mathematics Department and a Mining Department, which were joined in 1921-22 by the Departments of Naval Architecture and Pharmacy. The latter, eventually the largest pharmacy department in the country, began as a single bench in the Chemistry Department! Growth in quality was reflected in affiliation to the University of Durham in 1930, the establishment of the London University BSc Pharmacy in 1930, and recognition by that university of the college as a centre for its BEng in 1934. The Sunderland Technical College went from strength to strength and became a polytechnic in 1969 (only the third institution to be awarded that status) then a university in 1992 (a month after city status was awarded!). In the process it amalgamated with the School of Art and Sunderland Training College. The main campuses of the University of Sunderland are now on Chester Road and on the north riverside.

BISHOPWEARMOUTH GREEN TOWARDS THE CHURCH

'DRINK VAUX ALES & Stout. In bottle' the sign on the right reads on what appears to be the gable end of a garage. On the left are the old almshouses and to the right of the sign used to be the premises of Kent's Decorators and Glaziers. It is difficult to date but this is probably the 1920s. Bishopwearmouth was one of the original three settlements on the banks of the River Wear that merged to form modern Sunderland. The settlement was formed in AD 930, when Athelstan (the first king of England) granted the lands to the Bishop of Durham. The settlement on the opposite side of the river, Monkwearmouth, had been founded 250 years earlier. The lands on the south side of the river became known as Bishopwearmouth, a parish that covered around 20 square miles, encompassing settlements such as Ryhope and Silksworth – now part of the modern Sunderland urban area. Within the parish was another settlement, Sunderland, which was a small fishing port at the mouth of the river. Over the centuries, the port would grow in both importance and size, and in 1719 was made into a parish independent from Bishopwearmouth.

THE TREE GROWTH has obscured the scene now, but a church dedicated to St Michael has stood on this site for over a thousand years. For most of that time, it has been known as Bishopwearmouth parish church. The parish of Bishopwearmouth, south of the River Wear, was founded in AD 930, with an original stone church being built shortly afterwards. The first evidence of a church on the site arose in a 1930s excavation, when Saxon stones were found. Due to colliery subsidence, the church was virtually rebuilt beyond recognition in the early twentieth century. In 1998, following the grant of city status, the church was redesignated as Sunderland Minster: possibly the first Minster Church in England since the Reformation. In May 2007, with the adoption of Benedict Biscop as Sunderland's Patron Saint, the church was redesignated as an Extra Parochial Place with the addition of St Benedict Biscop in its title.

GREEN TERRACE AND THE END OF CHESTER ROAD

THE NAME IS obvious enough, but this was probably not the site of the original village green of Saxon Bishopwearmouth since it would be next to a burn and would, therefore, be liable to flooding. The original green was probably south-east of the Church of St Michael and on a distinct eminence, which is still so obvious today. Indeed, part of it survives and has been awarded a blue plaque. However, in Norman times and after the devastation of the North, the village was refounded and laid out along the broad street to the north, which was once known as 'The Square' or 'Front Street'. On the left are the premises of 'W. McKenzie Chimney Sweep'. The stone wall, which is mostly made of local magnesian limestone, features on the *Rain's Eye Plan* map developed by John Rain between 1785 and 1790, so the wall is probably a good deal older than that. Bishopwearmouth was a vast parish of over 9,000 acres even after Sunderland parish was cut out of it in 1719. By the 1820s and 1830s, one could say that there was a drift of the wealthier classes from Sunderland into less crowded, leafier and altogether more pleasant Bishopwearmouth.

THE GALEN BUILDING stands at the junction of Green Terrace and Albion Place today. In 1901, the municipal Technical College was opened near Bishopwearmouth Green. The decision was prompted by the possibility of funding under the Local Taxation and Customs and Excise Act of 1890. The Galen Building, original home of the Technical College, was paid for from so-called 'Whiskey Money' at a cost of £27,800. It was extended between 1922 and 1930, with both private and public funding, and later became part of the Sunderland Polytechnic and later the university. The old Galen Building has become a licensed bar of the Varsity chain. On the left is The Bridges multi-storey car park and the rear entrance to Debenhams is tucked in there as well. The old wall is still there though, supporting this section of Bishopwearmouth as it has since at least the earlier eighteenth century – and is indeed a listed wall now. Surprisingly, one of the oldest secular buildings in the city is the older part of FitzGerald's Wine Bar, which is just opposite. In 1785, that block of properties on the north side of Green Terrace also contained, among other things, a tannery and the Sunderland Workhouse.

HIGH STREET
FROM THE WEST

THIS IS A splendid scene, capturing a lot of action. The sign reads 'Caslaw, Hayter & Tate' late with Jopling & Tuer, Clothiers, Hatters and Mercers' and further down you could find Lutert's Ship Inn. A visitor to Sunderland in 1879 was particularly scathing about the amount of drinking which prevailed in High Street and remarked that 'Sunderland itself consists of one long street, narrow, and full of public houses ...' Down at the bottom of the bank is the covered market which was the Metro Centre of its day and even had a fairground run by the Duke family, where troublesome children could be whirled and shaken into

submission; the market closed in the 1930s after a century of supplying the needs of East End folk. On the right is Sans Street Mission. Twin, parallel 'ribbons' can be seen clearly through the cobbles – they made it easier for the horses to pull their loads up the street on wagons or 'rolleys', and extra horses known as 'chain' horses could be coupled on to help. They would often be sisal loads on their way to Craven's Ropeworks in Roker Avenue.

THE PARTNERSHIP OF Thomas Jopling and Joseph Tuer was the beginning of the longest established department store in Sunderland. In 1804, they opened a drapery business at 174-178 High Street East. From 1882, it traded as Hedley, Swan & Co., but the store was known as Jopling's. By 1900, they had one hundred employees. The ground floor housed ready-made and tailored clothing for gentlemen and one could find ladies' clothing, along with household furniture and the tailors' workrooms on the first floor. By 1919, Jopling's had expanded so much that they had to move to bigger premises and the move was made to the top of High Street West, which was the heart of the town's commercial district. Sadly, there was a fire on the night of Tuesday, 14 December 1954 which completely destroyed the store and all of the contents, but Jopling's were back in business within six weeks at the original premises on High Street East. The new four-storey department store in John Street was completed and opened for business in May 1956, with Sunderland's first escalator built in. The oldest department store in Sunderland closed in 2010 when Jopling's went into administration.

CORNER OF HIGH STREET AND VILLIERS STREET

AT THE TIME of its development in the early nineteenth century, this was a high-class residential area made up of large houses with coach houses at the rear. It was one of the first streets to be paved under the 1809 Sunderland Improvement Act. The Villiers Electric Theatre was in Villiers Street, Hendon and was the first purpose-built cinema in Sunderland, which was opened on 2 January 1912 at a cost of £4,000 and held 1,000 patrons. The first film shown in 1912 was *The Great Mine Disaster* and the last was the Disney film *Rob Roy* starring Richard Todd on 16 March 1958, when the cinema

closed its doors. The Lambton Bank on the left was once the premises of Harrison's wholesale suppliers of hardware such as nuts, screws, washers and bolts etc. In the right foreground is an electricity feeder pillar from which a network of cables will lead. Seen on the left side of Villiers Street is the tall building that was once Ditchburn's furniture store. 'Jack' Ditchburn was the 'banker' of the famous Sunderland AFC 'Bank of England' team. Those were the days!

THE RATHER ARISTOCRATIC name is derived from Lady Ann Barbara Frances Villiers, wife of the wealthy coal owner William Henry Lambton (father of the first Earl of Durham) who owned the land. In fact, she was the daughter of the infamous Lady Jersey, who was one of the mistresses of George IV. While on the subject of street names it is worth pointing out that Sunderland, like many other towns, has a 'High Street' and that normally refers to commercial significance. In Sunderland's case there is a Low Street running parallel to it and High Street is literally considerably higher. Originally, in the days before the Wearmouth Bridge was built, the main commercial axis of the town was High Street but when the bridge was built there began a process whereby the main commercial thoroughfares became Fawcett Street and Bridge Street. The City Traffic Department can achieve a similar but much quicker effect with a couple of cunningly positioned traffic lights and a bus lane! Of course nowadays Fawcett Street in turn has been sadly reduced by the impact of The Bridges and out-of-town shopping malls.

THE EXCHANGE BUILDING AND LOWER END OF HIGH STREET EAST

IT WAS A Mr Newbiggin who, in the 1860s, established the Eagle Tavern and the Eagle Tobacco Factory surmounted by a huge eagle replica. The former was described by family historian, James Watson Corder, as 'never an inn of interest or good class'. The property was taken over by Fairgreaves electrical engineering firm before the First World War and they were the first firm in the UK to manufacture Bakelite, from 1913. The Exchange Building stands further down. War with France (1793-1815) stimulated the economy of

Sunderland and it was believed that an Exchange Building would be essential for the future prosperity of the expanding township. The slum area of the Half Moon estate was the preferred site and a prospectus was published showing that the building was to have brokers' offices, a newsroom and a post office etc. Shares at £50 each were taken up for the building, which cost £8,000. The first stone was laid on 10 August 1812 by Sir Henry Vane Tempest and it was completed and opened to the public on 10 May 1814. The 'chaste, elegant structure' was designed by John Stokoe of Newcastle and built by George Cameron, grandfather of inventor Joseph Swan.

BY THE 1880s, the Exchange had fallen into decay leaving 'a heavy dull stone building, for some years almost deserted'. In 1889, it became the base of the Seamen's Mission whose efforts were described by the East End Commission as 'touching very closely the life of the district'. By the 1990s, it was no more than a shell when it became the scene of a case which occupied national headlines on and off for many months. Nikki Allan, a seven-year-old girl, was murdered on Wear Garth estate in Sunderland and her body was found outside the Exchange Building. There was a clamour for the demolition of the Exchange, but fortunately the Tyne and Wear Development Corporation restored it and it is now in use as a hotel and wine bar. The original 6.5ft-high golden eagle is now in exile on the island of Jersey following a long sojourn in a builder's yard in Deptford, so what now surmounts the restored Eagle Tavern property is a replica of a replica eagle! Fairgrieves Mouldings is still very much in operation but now in Washington.

SUNDERLAND PARISH CHURCH

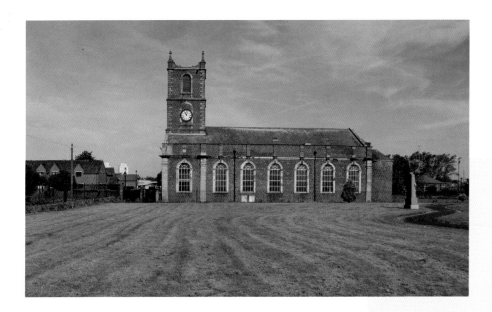

HOLY TRINITY CHURCH was designed possibly by Nicholas Hawksmoor or William Etty of York, built in 1719 and consecrated in September that year by the Bishop of London. It was built because of the rising population in the Port of Sunderland area. Within the church were rooms for civic functions – a courtroom, meeting place for the vestry, and later a library. Streets of new houses soon surrounded the church to the north and west, although to the south and east the town moor remained an open space. In 1803, Thomas Wilson, schoolmaster turned engineer and architect of the original Wearmouth Bridge, supervised the renewal of the roof and several windows. Because of the growing population the cemetery was extended on many occasions and covered five acres, making it the largest enclosed churchyard outside of London. There were burials there from 1719 to 1901. Over 75,000 people were buried there. The last burial was in 1901. George Garbutt, family historian, when describing the many tombs and headstones before him, was moved to remark 'that in the reflections suggested by a contemplation of the many memorials of mortality, we are made sensible of the short and transitory state of human existence'.

AS THE POPULATION of the old East End of Sunderland moved westwards, the congregation became too reduced to be able to maintain the fabric of the church. It is now a Grade I listed building that has been looked after by the Churches Conservation Trust since 1988 and Sunderland Old Township Heritage Society. It is still used for services six times a year. In Church Street East a few of the grand houses from this time still stand, and along Church Walk a later eighteenth-century school, the famous Donnison School, and the Trafalgar Almshouses of the 1840s. The church is used for a range of events such as concerts, art and photographic exhibitions, and summer and Christmas fairs – very much in the tradition of churches being community centres as well as places of worship. The parish of Sunderland which was served by the church is no more than 178 acres in extent – of which originally 58 acres were tidal waters and 20 acres were town moor and churchyard. This, associated with an expanding population in the earlier nineteenth century, resulted in severe public health problems and mortality rates well above the average. Indeed, the area is still categorised as deprived.

RIVER SCENE LOOKING DOWNSTREAM FROM THE WEARMOUTH BRIDGE

WILSONS SAW MILL is on the riverside on the left and was famous for the unusual 'House on Stilts'. Also visible are the chimneys and warehouses of Deuchar's Brewery. The three tugs belonged to the Lambton, Hetton and Joicey Collieries and are distinguishable from those of France Fenwick because they have three horizontal rings on their funnels, while the latter had stripes. There were the Lumley, Eppleton Hall and Houghton tugs that met colliers to bring them back to the staiths and through the rigging of the middle vessel Bonnersfield can be seen. Bonnersfield is shown on *Rain's Eye Plan* (1785) and was occupied at that time by a

large brewery and raff yard, owned by John Stafford and Cooper Abbs. The name derives from a Mr Bonner, who owned a raff or timber yard on the site. Eventually it was the site of the brewery and bonded warehouses and in its later stages there was a firm making looms there. Above the smoke is Dickinson's Engine Works which produced marine engines and to the right of that is Manor Quay, where J.L. Thompson's fitted out 'floats' (meaning that ships were completed and berthed).

ALONG THE MODERN riverside there is a block of luxury flats, the university riverside campus and then the National Glass Centre. This area especially represents the trauma of the closure of the last shipyards during the premiership of Margaret Thatcher. Sunderland was one of the areas selected to be involved in the regeneration programme of the Tyne and Wear Development Corporation (TWDC), which was established in 1987 to develop land on the banks of the River Tyne and the River Wear in England. Its flagship developments included the regeneration of the East Quayside in Newcastle, Royal Quays in North Tyneside and the St Peter's area in Sunderland, but it was dissolved in 1998. The legacy of TWDC remains controversial within the region, in particular in Sunderland, where it is believed the investment in services and leisure opportunities in Newcastle, where the Corporation was based, was not matched in the rest of the region. The Corporation also invested heavily in developing the Tyne and Wear Metro system, although this was not extended to Sunderland until after the Corporation was shut down.

NORTH SANDS
(PALMERS QUAY)
TOWARDS THE BRIDGES

THIS IMAGE SHOWS the east end of Dickinson's Engine Works and the west end of the
Manor Quay. Donkey boilers worked the cranes and other equipment. On the left one can
see what looks, at first glance, like a huge, toothed machine but it is actually just a gangway
that would have been raised to reach the side of incoming vessels. Lambton, Hetton and
Joicey tugs can be seen in the picture as well as a little cart, or bogey, with iron wheels,
and very large 'pails' in the middle foreground which were the equivalent of today's skips.

Beyond them one can see a large bench with a vice attached to it.
The scene sings riverside industrial activity and will have had the
distinctive smell of acrid smoke, steam, paint and paraffin. Waples
took photographs of many industrial scenes like this with no
obvious motive other than to record change, or just because he was a
compulsive clicker.

THE FIRST BRIDGE was opened in 1796 and this photograph (left)
shows the third and current Wearmouth Bridge to be located here.
There was originally a toll for traffic and pedestrians, although the
latter was abolished in 1846. It was the second iron bridge built after
the famous span at Ironbridge, but twice as long and cost £28,000.
From 1857 to 1859 it was reconstructed by Robert Stephenson, who
stripped it back to its six iron ribs and levelled the hump by raising
the abutments. The bridge reopened in March 1859, with the toll
completely abolished in 1885. To accommodate the growing volume
of traffic, construction began on the current bridge in 1927 and was
designed by Mott, Hay & Anderson, and fabricated by Sir William
Arrol & Co. at their Dalmarnock Ironworks in Glasgow (they also built
the famous Forth Rail Bridge and the steel structure of Tower Bridge
in London). The new bridge was built around the old one to allow the
road to remain open to traffic. The Duke of York (later King George VI)
opened the new bridge on 31 October 1929. The railway bridge was
built in 1879 and extended the railway south from Monkwearmouth
to the centre of Sunderland.

THE RIVERSIDE
AT LOW QUAY

THE MODERN FISH QUAY is here. In the background is the Scotia Engine Works. On the right on the north side of the river is the Manor Quay and J.L. Thompson's fitting-out quay. The ferry landing steps are on the north side. On the left is a dredging hopper and the two tugs with the striped sections on their funnels were originally built and operated by Hepple & Co. of South Shields for the Lambton, Hetton & Joicey Collieries Ltd. The tug on the right is a paddle tug, but she is moored next to a screw tug. Another of the group was the *Eppleton Hall* which worked originally from Tyne Dock but later transferred to

Sunderland. The tugs were sold to France Fenwick, Tyne & Wear Ltd when the pits were nationalised in 1947. Fenwick & Co. was a shipping company engaged in the Australian wool trade from 1834 and later in the East Coast coal trade. William France also owned colliers in 1901. During the early part of the twentieth century, they built up a fleet of deep-sea tramps in addition to their colliers, but both trades were in severe recession by 1975 and the company was 'wound up'.

IN 1964, THE last paddle tugs were decommissioned and sold to Seaham Harbour Dock Co. The *Eppleton Hall* was restored in 1969-70 and crossed the Atlantic then via the Panama Canal to serve as the yacht of Karl Kortum, director of San Francisco Maritime Museum. She was later given to the USA National Park Service in 1979 and is berthed in San Francisco. In 1879, the River Wear Commissioners (RWC) built a new fish quay and market inside the South Outlet on the north side of the Hendon Channel entrance to Hendon Dock. In 1883, new covered facilities were introduced, together with the replacement of independent fish sellers by an official seller appointed by the RWC. This decision led to great animosity towards the RWC by independent sellers and many local fishermen. Hendon Channel fish quay was closed when a blockship was sunk across the South Outlet pier ends at the start of the First World War. The Fish Quay was then relocated to Thornhill Quay, moving further upstream in 1931 to make way for the new Corporation Quay. It has been located at its current site since July 1939.

LOW QUAY

THE FERRY STEPS are just off the picture to the right. At the end of the houses to the left and just around the corner was the birthplace of the famous Jack Crawford, the keelman (probably of Scottish ancestry) who nailed the Admiral's flag back to the mast at Camperdown in 1797 and contributed to the glorious victory over a Dutch fleet. In this picture, the tide is out and the sticky black 'sleck' at the base of the quay would have been covered when the tide came in, with the cobbles floating. This is quite a significant picture in fact, because it shows work on the creation of the new Deep Water or Corporation Quay in the early 1930s. The houses at the east end of the row are being demolished (look at the roofs!). A jetty has been run out so that the hopper can continue to be loaded and there is a crane with a donkey engine at the entrance to the South Dock. Also visible is the original dock head office.

IN OCTOBER 1934, Sir John Priestman opened the new Corporation Quay. From 1941 it played a major role in the war effort by shipping war materials. Later, thousands of tons of US Army stores were landed there and after the war, efforts were made to restore pre-war cargo liner services. British India, Union Castle, Ellerman and Clan Line vessels regularly discharged cargoes of chrome ore and sisal (for ropes) from East Africa. Other cargoes, including timber, wood pulp, pit props, esparto grass and general goods contributed greatly to tonnage handled. With the long-term decline of the North East's traditional industries hitting staple trades, containerisation seemed to provide part of the solution. The first of such shipments at Corporation Quay was discharged from the motor vessel *Nordsee* during September 1978. From 1979, the German shipping company Rheinmass used the quay for their UK-Nigeria service, but the civil war in Nigeria brought a close to the Baco–Liner service from the port. Although intermittent, some feeder vessels are still collecting and transporting containers, but most of this trade has now dried up. Direct trade links were established with Japan in 1987, with deliveries of huge cargoes of machinery for Nissan's factory being made.

CORPORATION QUAY – FORMERLY THE CUSTOM HOUSE QUAY

THE BOARS HEAD public house stands up on the right and the High Street Wesleyan Chapel is also visible. The old stone Elizabethan Customs House stands yards away from its new supplanter HM Customs & Excise Warehouses and Office. Behind the house on the left is Dean's Yard and a veritable warren of dark alleys and passageways. Beyond them is the lower end of High Street East. The mast or pole is not a telegraph pole, but is likely to be some sort of signaling device. It is not at all clear why the men are crowded on and above the ferry landing steps. The area was cleared in 1932 for the construction of Corporation Quay, which was opened on 9 October 1934. The need for a deep-water riverside quay to accommodate large cargo ships had long been recognised before the town council obtained statutory powers to build it in 1927. It was at the onset of the Great Depression of the 1930s and the accompanying large-scale unemployment, which provided impetus to begin the project that would secure work for local labour.

EXCAVATION WORK STARTED in October 1930, involving the demolition of an area which had once formed part of 'Old Sunderland's' waterfront. Under the supervision of the RWC's engineer, Mr W.H.S. Tripp, construction of the quay was undertaken by Peter Lind & Co. Ltd of London, during which twenty-six huge concrete pillars were sunk into the river frontage to support the quay platform. A retaining wall, some 40ft high, was also built to support High Street East, which runs above the rear of the quay. A two-storey reinforced concrete warehouse and transit shed, 300ft long by 75ft wide, was built by Stewart Partners Ltd. Two miles of railway track was laid and three 5-ton quayside cranes were erected. The provision of coal and oil bunkering facilities also helped to stimulate the Wear's ship repair industry and the first ship to berth at Corporation Quay was Royal Mail Lines' 9,409-ton cargo liner, *Lochkatrine*, which arrived from Rotterdam on 1 June 1934, to load binding twine and fertiliser for Vancouver – four months before the official opening ceremony.

THE GRAVING DOCK UNDER THE RAILWAY BRIDGE

THE CLASSIC FORM of dry dock, or graving dock, is a narrow basin usually made of earthen berms and concrete, closed by gates or by a caisson, into which a vessel may be floated and the water pumped out, leaving the vessel supported on blocks. More routine use of dry docks is for the cleaning and repainting of ships' hulls. This dock was owned by Robert Thompson's, a company that fitted out ships, for some time. The quayside building

probably contains a band-saw and other equipment. The dock is angled so it will have been difficult to get ships into it. Under the bridges at Panns Bank one can see S.P. Austin's Shipbuilders & Ship Repairers in pre-pontoon days. The firm was started by Peter Austin at North Sands in 1826 and moved to the south bank in 1846. The pontoon, or floating dock, was opened and commissioned in 1903 on the site of the bottleworks which had previously occupied the riverside there. It was capable of taking vessels of up to 400ft in length and was a tremendous asset to the company, but S.P. Austin closed in 1967. On the right horizon is St Mary's Roman Catholic Church.

THE RIVERSIDE AREA opposite was the original heart of Sunderland industry because the production of sea salt began there in the late sixteenth century, hence the name Pann Lane, which commemorates the use of big iron troughs, or pans, to boil the saltwater in. The original Wearmouth Bridge, sponsored and at least in part designed by the banker Rowland Burdon, had been opened in 1796. It was not, in truth, very robust and had to be greatly strengthened in 1805, in case it fell down! Then in 1857-59, it was totally rebuilt by Robert Stephenson who used the ribs of the original bridge, albeit disguised by the insertion of new wrought-iron arches. The abutments were raised as well, so that the distinctive hump of the original bridge was eliminated. Stephenson's bridge was joined by the railway bridge in 1879, but until then there were two separate railway networks on either side of the river. In 1879, the NER closed the gap and linked Monkwearmouth with Ryhope Grange. The bridge was designed by Thomas Harrison and in its day it was the largest single-arched hog-backed iron-girder bridge in the world.

BRIDGE STREET FROM MACKIE'S CORNER

HAVING FOLLOWED A circuit around the town centre, Holmeside and High Street West, this is the point at which we will cross the river. This photo (below) looks like the 1940s or later. Walker's Jewellers are on the left, then Milburn's Bakers on a little bit from there and then St Mary's Church further down. On the other side of the road is the Grand Hotel. 'Travellers and tourists arriving at this busy Wearside centre will be well advised in making their headquarters during a brief or prolonged stay at the handsome and commodious establishment recently opened under the style of the "Grand Hotel", and which offers perfectly up-to-date accommodation for either commercial or family visits to the town. Centrally situated within one minute's walk of the railway station, the "Grand" has an imposing front elevation of five storeys'. This advert in the 1902 Coronation Souvenir also drew careful attention to the fact that 'the sanitary arrangements are completely in accordance with the

latest scientific improvements'. The hotel was used by the Admiralty during the Second World War. The well-known Share's Furniture Store is next to it and there were also two opticians in this street – Emerson's and Haig's. Just look at the pram in the centre of the picture, which appears to have two babies in it!

THE GRAND HOTEL building in Bridge Street was one of the town's main hotels until its closure in 1969 and had fifty bedrooms. It was bought by Berni Inns Ltd, which planned a major reconstruction of the building. After Berni was merged with Grand Metropolitan Hotels in 1970, the hotel was offered for sale but failed to attract a buyer, leaving it to fall into a dilapidated state and it was later demolished to be replaced by Bridge House, a block of offices available for rent. Further down on the right, at 14 Bridge Street, were the offices of the *Sunderland Echo*, into which it moved in July 1876 and where it remained for the next 100 years. News of a move from Bridge Street to Pennywell, Sunderland, was announced during the anniversary celebrations in 1973 and the old building has since been replaced by a modern apartment block. St Mary's Roman Catholic Church was designed in the Gothic style by the important Durham architect Ignatius Bonomi (1787-1870) and reflects the increasing tolerance and prosperity experienced by Catholics after legal restrictions on their faith had been lifted in 1829. This grandeur, however, is reserved for the façade as the rest of the building was executed in rough local magnesium limestone.

WEARMOUTH BRIDGE FROM THE END OF BRIDGE STREET

THIS VIEW IS over the old bridge built by Robert Stephenson and looking towards North Bridge Street. Just next to it was the Trustees Savings Bank. The Monkwearmouth Picture Hall, converted from the former St Stephen's Presbyterian Chapel, was opened in May 1906 by George Black and was the first permanent cinema in the town. The disused chapel was originally home to Black's Waxworks Exhibition. Picture shows were put on there as early as 1904 and the cinema was run by George Black Senior and his three sons, who made up The Blacks Animated Picture Company. In 1919, it was taken over by Will Marshall and was

named Bromarsh – a composite of Marshall Brothers. Sadly, it was destroyed by enemy bombs in 1943. Beyond the Bromarsh is the 'Scotch Church' (Presbyterian), with the Aquatic Arms and Royal Hotel in the centre of the image. The Aquatic was run for a long time by the parents of footballer Arthur Housam. The portico of the Monkwearmouth Station is quite clear, with its goods yard behind it and fleets of three-wheeled Scammel trucks that would distribute from there on a daily basis. The original toll house is on the left. Wheelbarrows like the one seen here could be hired for 6d a day from Harts of Norfolk Street.

MONKWEARMOUTH STATION MUSEUM opened in 1973 to preserve the neoclassical station building, and to provide displays of transport and local history. The station was designed by Thomas Moore of Sunderland and opened in 1848 as the Sunderland terminus for trains from Gateshead and Newcastle. It closed in 1967 and was bought by the Corporation for conversion into a museum and this included restoration of the original booking office, which had remained unchanged since 1866. In recent years, the museum has widened its role to cater more for family groups, in particular for children under five, and has received national and local commendations for its work with young children. The Tyne & Wear Metro and mainline trains still pass through the station without stopping, but the Metro calls at St Peter's station a few hundred yards south of the old station. It is part of the Tyne & Wear Museums group and is a Grade II* listed building. From 1928, the famous London Palladium was managed by George Black Junior and was even a cinema for three months, but during the 1930s it became the regular home for The Crazy Gang. Black controlled the large Moss Empires group of theatres.

NORTH BRIDGE STREET LOOKING TOWARDS THE WHEATSHEAF

THE WHEATSHEAF INN was built in 1904 on the site of an earlier coaching inn. The lighthouse was a wooden folly which was a replica of the octagonal lighthouse that stood on the North Pier until 1902. There was a light, but it was not allowed to be used because it could be misinterpreted from the sea as a genuine navigation light. It was the emblem of Wills Lighthouse Stores, which was originally to be found within; the firm was a wholesale and retail grocers, and provision merchants. Later on the building was occupied by Walter Willsons and its final occupant, in the 1950s, was Marley's sweetshop with its myriads of tantalising glass jars full of sweets. The old DSS offices stood on the left and on the right one could find Smith's Furniture Store, running from

Dundas Street. Over to the right, next to the Wheatsheaf Inn, was the tram/bus depot. The man pictured on the left with the cow's bottom looks as though he has walked off the set of the 1962 version of *Jack the Giant Killer* and is probably escorting it to slaughter houses. On the pavement to the left is a small group of schoolgirls and one of them seems to be carrying a domestic science basket.

THE CORPORATION WAS authorised to operate motorbuses in 1927 and the first service, a tram replacement route serving the docks area, commenced on 6 February 1928. It was not until May 1929 that Sunderland Corporation took delivery of its own motorbuses. Throughout the 1930s, the motorbus network continued to expand with the new estates built at Ford, Marley Potts, Plains Farm, Pallion, Fulwell and Seaburn being served by new bus routes. Although motorbuses had been introduced, the tramway system continued to be extended and in 1937 the Fulwell Lane route was extended east to Seaburn via Dykelands Road. In 1948, the Durham Road line was extended along a central reservation to Grindon Lane and the following year to Thorney Close Road to serve the new housing estates there. However, the decision had already been taken to abandon the tramway system in favour of motorbuses and on 5 November 1950 the Villette Road–Suffolk Road loop line was closed, and on 30 November the following year the Southwick route closed. Remaining routes survived until 1954, before they were gradually run down over the course of that year and the system finally closed amidst great ceremony on 1 October 1954, with the No. 86 the last tram to make its journey.

ST PETER'S CHURCH

A MONASTERY WAS founded in AD 674 by Benedict Biscop at Monkwearmouth on land given by Egfrid, King of Northumbria. His idea was to build a model monastery for England in the Roman tradition in an area previously more influenced by Celtic Christianity. A papal letter in AD 678 exempted the monastery from external control, and in AD 682 the king was so delighted at the success of St Peter's that he gave Benedict more land in Jarrow and urged him to build a second monastery. Benedict brought workmen from Francia to build these churches, the first ecclesiastical structures in Britain built of stone, and furnished with glass windows, pictures, service books and the library he had collected on his travels. Window glass being unusual in England at the time, Benedict imported glassmakers from Francia who established a workshop at the Monkwearmouth site, near the River Wear. Benedict was the first abbot, and the monastery flourished under him and his successors for 200 years. Before his death, Benedict stipulated that the two sites should function as 'one monastery in two places'. Hallgarth Square is beyond the church.

IN 1545 'ALL the house and seite of the late cell of Monkwearmouth', valued at £26 yearly, were granted by Henry VIII to Thomas Whitehead. Monkwearmouth passed afterwards to the Widdrington family then the Fenwicks. The monastic remains were incorporated into a private mansion built in James I's reign, but this burnt down in 1790 and there is no longer any visible trace of the monastery. The houses which once stood south of the church were known as Hallgarth. As a result of the dumping of ballast, by the late eighteenth century the old church was surrounded by sandhills that left the church lying in a hollow, rather than standing on a slope, when they were removed. The gravestones were cleared away at a later date, although several of the more interesting ones lie near the steps by the vicarage. Professor Rosemary Cramp conducted a famous archaeological excavation here in the 1950s, which revealed the layout of the ancient monastery. She recalled the interest shown by the residents of Hallgarth Square, which was a very poor area in slum conditions at that time.

THE WHEATSHEAF JUNCTION

THIS PICTURE WAS taken at the intersection of Newcastle Road and Southwick Road. The Wheatsheaf Hall at the bottom of Southwick Road and the corner of the Wheatsheaf was taken over by Lough & Richardson in 1906. A year later James Tindle

took it over and renamed it the Wheatsheaf Picture Hall, then later the Coronation Picture Palace, after the Coronation of George V – it became known as the 'Cora' and was run by Tindle's son, James Junior, from 1911 to 1948. James Junior also owned a fleet of charabancs and the father of actress Christine Norden (mistress of Alexander Korda) was one of his drivers. Christine Norden played the piano in the cinema to accompany the silent movies. The second smallest cinema in Sunderland, it was known as a 'flea pit' – it certainly had to be disinfected by the council in 1930. It closed in 1959 and was demolished in 1982. Next to the Wheatsheaf was a blacksmith and cartwright's business owned by W.H. Sutton. Off to the left was the Wearmouth Colliery School and the building can still be found there today.

THE WHEATSHEAF public house is just off the picture on the far right (above) and is one of Sunderland's most prominent landmarks north of the Wear. The impressive design is a rebuilding of a smaller pub that had occupied the site since 1828. It was a simple three-storey building that stood at the junction of six roads. However, Newcastle Breweries wanted to make better use of the prominent site and commissioned Joseph Oswald (1851-1930) to design a replacement. Oswald was the son of the prolific Newcastle architect, Septimus Oswald; he became a partner in his father's firm in 1876 and assumed control of the practice when his father died in 1894. An expert in the design of pubs, Oswald was involved in the development of over 100 such buildings in the region, including the Beehive Inn in Newcastle and the Blue Bell Hotel at Roker. A particularly impressive example of his work was the head office of Newcastle Breweries in Newcastle (1896-1901), with its vibrant interior in turquoise and yellow faience.

THE BATHING BEACH AND THE ROKER AND SOUTH BREAKWATERS

A ROW OF bathing huts on the beach between the piers gave rise to the name of the 'Bathing Beach'. As well as the huts, there was also a floating diving board. The developers of the Roker Hotel had visions of this area as the nucleus of a spa resort, and the hotel was so-called because the owner pumped sea water into the building to provide hot and cold showers and steam-vapour baths. It was believed that saltwater was good for the constitution. This aspiration to become akin to Brighton is commemorated now only in the name Roker Baths Road. At this time, Smith's donkeys were stabled behind the Roker Hotel and later they were

in stables adjacent to St Benet's Church. When the donkeys' working day was done, small boys flocked to volunteer to take them back to their stables but of course, this was just a ploy to get a free ride, because the donkeys were so practiced in their routine that they were quite capable of returning to their stables by themselves. They could probably have collected the money and made cream teas too given the chance.

SUNDERLAND'S HARBOUR WAS created around 1717, when the River Wear Commissioners were established, and the two inner piers date back to the eighteenth century. The great North Breakwater was a long time in coming, but RWC engineers had been proposing such a development since the mid-eighteenth century and in 1876, a thorough report on the subject proposed two breakwaters. Work finally began in 1885. Advantage was taken of a natural rock outcrop as a foundation, but a foundation of rubble and cement had to be embedded further out. The huge blocks were put in place using a 290-ton hydraulic crane. Along the whole length was a tunnel to carry the cables and act as maintenance access in bad conditions. The final blocks were put in place in 1902, with one being laid by Ferdinand de Lesseps, builder of the Suez Canal, who visited Roker in 1889. The 2,800ft-long breakwater was opened in September 1903. Work started on the South Breakwater in 1893, but with trade and RWC income in decline before the First World War, it was decided to cut back on the original plan for twin breakwaters and to conclude work on the South Breakwater in 1912.

75

ROKER BEACH FROM NEAR THE COASTGUARD'S HUT

THIS IS A rather spectacular picture (right), but Waples' caption reads simply '10.30'. This is probably a bank holiday and the fashions are of the 1920s. People dressed up to go to the seaside in those days and even the swimming costumes reveal little! Some of the costumes are draped over the tops of the tents to dry out. The tide is up, it is mid-morning and there is little room unoccupied. There is a roof advert for Notarianni's, which was owned by Benedetto Notarianni, who was born in 1892 in Valvori in Southern Italy and died in 1962. He emigrated from Italy to Glasgow in 1900 to work in his uncle's café, although he went back to his home country to fight in the Great War, returning to the UK with his brothers. After his marriage in 1923 he moved to Sunderland and opened his first shop in Silksworth Row, which he eventually sold to his brother Luigi, and opened an ice-cream parlour in High Street West. In 1938, he moved again to the opposite side of High Street West and this famous parlour closed

in 1988. He also opened the shop at Seaburn and in the 1960s opened the Bis-Bar in Park Lane in the town centre.

THE ADJACENT ROKER Ravine contains some fine caves and is itself a collapsed cavern. Further incursion was stopped by the building of the Roker Low Promenade. The road bridge was built as late as 1880 and it was only then that the development of the seafront, in the form of fine terraced housing built on Williamson land, could begin. Before the stone road bridge was built the route to Whitburn was via Cleadon. At a later date the rather ornate building beyond the beach shelter became the Rococo Nightclub and it is now the Smugglers Inn. Nowadays, the sands of Roker and Seaburn are nothing like as busy as they were into the 1950s and it is not easy to understand the part they played in the social life of the town. For those of us who remember, it seems like a Golden Age dominated by square, green canvas tents, banana-and-sand sandwiches, the taste of very salty sea water and queues of people at Seaburn Camp waiting for the bus, or at the tram shelter across the road from Alex Hasting's at the end of another hard day on the beach.

HOLEY ROCK

IN THE BACKGROUND is Holey Rock. This was a 'stack' in development – eventually the caves would collapse, leaving a freestanding pillar like others along the coast. From the front it resembled an elephant, which is why it was also known as Elephant Rock. Probably as a result of a popular misinterpretation of the origin of the name, there was a tendency to keep pieces of the rock as charms against the power of witches. For those who believe in such things, it is advisable to collect a couple of those curious stones on the beach with holes bored through them by a rather strange sea creature and to tie a ribbon through the hole. Supposedly this guarantees protection against an assortment of the usual types of spells and also from toothache. Pierrots were self-employed entertainers who let the public see snatches of their show as 'trailers' and a group of them performed near here, during

the summer season before 1914. Not much is known about these artists, but one of them was Theobald Vickery of a Somerset family who, around 1880, moved to Sunderland where they had relatives and lived in Gladstone Street. It may be that other members of the family took part in the Pierrots too.

OF COURSE THE holes of Holey Rock, from which it derived its name, held a great fascination for children, who would try to race backwards and forwards through them to see if they could beat the waves of the incoming tide. The caves were potentially dangerous because the rising tide would fill them up to the height of the dark band on the stone. Children played in the dank and dripping caves at low tide, but they were also the home to gambling schools of local card sharps as the flat sands outside were a good vantage point for uninterrupted observation of possible police raids. In a trice the gamblers could become innocent trippers and 'plodgers'. In 1930, it was decided that the honeycomb of holes and caves, together with small boys intrepidly climbing up the loose and tumbling rocks, was a recipe for disaster, so a plan was initiated to fill the caves with concrete. However, work did not begin on building a new retaining wall until 1936, which eventually extended round Roker Beach and involved demolishing the main Holey Rock. So that was the end of that stack!

SEABURN PROMENADE FROM THE NORTH

TENTS AND DECKCHAIRS could be hired at the north end of Seaburn promenade. The tents were put up for users and they would obviously prefer the ones nearest the water. Prices soared around 1930 and private-hire companies were accused of exploiting the public (presumably the summer weather was more reliable then). The *Sunderland Echo* insisted that the Corporation take over the job and end the monopoly, leading to the Corporation taking over responsibility for the beaches in 1934 – they purchased 300 tents and 2,000 deckchairs for public use. Prices were fixed at a certain rate and the tents came in three sizes with prices between sixpence (2.5p) and one shilling and sixpence (7.5p). The tents had big pockets stitched into the bottom so that sand and rocks could be piled in to try and stabilise them in winds. For an extra threepence you could hire a deckchair or card table. There were people who made an income for themselves by taking the tents back on behalf of the hirers and obtaining the deposit as payment. If you couldn't afford a tent you had to perform a striptease beneath a towel, which could go dramatically wrong. 'Sandscratchers' made a living by finding money lost on the beach or items which could be sold.

THERE WAS CONTROVERSY in the 1930s with regards to the council's policy of trying to attract visitors from the wider North East and a similar debate is had today regarding the International Air Show. In 1930, one Seaburn tradesman remarked, 'We do not want to attract large crowds of day-trippers who bring little or no advantage to the town at the expense of our own townspeople who are not able to enjoy the seaside amenities to the same extent as before. The other day I saw twelve charabanc trips come into Seaburn. They all had food and drink with them. They spent the day on the beach and probably never spent a penny with a Sunderland shopkeeper'. The end of Sunderland as a significant long-stay regional holiday resort came from a combination of rising incomes and aspirations, and new travel opportunities. By the late 1950s and '60s, cheap package holidays provided the first chance for most people in the United Kingdom to have affordable travel abroad. On the other hand, Sunderland still appeals to short-term tourism because it is a good base with easy access to the surrounding region and because of its vast events calendar.

TENTLAND AT SEABURN

THE BEACH AREA around the Cat and Dog Stairs was 'the posh end', and that at the Sea Lane stretch was known as 'Tentland'. To get the best possible pitch for the day, members of the family would get to the beach as early as possible to hold an area of sand to accommodate those following behind, with dad carrying the tent. This photo (below) is from the 1920s or '30s judging from the women's clothing. Since the tents were usually in fairly standard colours – light green or off-white – they could not be easily distinguished. For small children emerging from the sea it was easy to lose track of their home tent and in the case of small boys, the situation was worsened by having to hang onto waterlogged, knitted swimming trunks at the same time. The Lost Children Kiosk was a busy place as frantic parents were reunited with tear-stained, sandy offspring. Between April and October of 1950 the twin resorts dealt with 750 cases of lost children and there were

1,758 first-aid casualties, including five dog bites, one donkey bite, fifteen jellyfish stings, five people were kicked by donkeys and ninety-eight people had sand cleared from their eyes. This was during a busy period, of course.

POST-WAR RECOVERY was slow although the Corporation produced an ambitious 'master plan'. The growth of the visitors to Seaburn did justify the work, but the Corporation was trying to develop the resort without spending much money! However, there were new attractions such as a roller-skating rink, a fairground and events such as the Durham County Agricultural Show in 1947. In 1949, Seaburn and Roker were classified as an official resort, which increased the allocation of sweets to seafront tradesmen! In the 1950s, the super kiosks were opened and the lawns and flower beds were developed. Later on in the 1970s, the Sea World Dolphinarium was opened, but by then the decline in visits had begun. Although the crowds have reduced, Sunderland continues to be a popular destination with about 9.9 million tourism visits per year, albeit heavily dominated by short, day visits. This generates about £342 million in city income and supports approximately 5,000 jobs. Of course long, consistent spells of sunny weather can still result in the swarming onto the beaches of the twin resorts, but without the forest of green and dirty-grey square tents which continue to live on in nostalgic memories!

CHESTER ROAD FROM THE ROYALTY INN

CHESTER ROAD IS one of those obvious locational street names and is probably so-called because it connected Sunderland to Chester-le-Street, which, until the late eighteenth century (when the first Wearmouth Bridge was built), had the lowest bridge over the Wear and was, therefore, an important thoroughfare. It was once known as Chester Lane and that is how it appears on early maps of the area. Similarly, the parallel Hylton Road was significant because it led to the Hylton Ferry. The Royalty Theatre is just beyond the houses on the left and it looks very much as though the houses on the right are being demolished as the road is being widened. There are electric street lighting columns. In some cases the 'gallery' was hooked on and would swing in the wind. The low-level railway bridge was part of the system linking Sunderland Station to Millfield, Pallion and then Cox Green and Durham. Chester Road Board School can be seen beyond that on the left.

THE ROYALTY STANDS where the coal wagons from surrounding mines would begin to cross Church-owned land in order to reach ships waiting for them on the river. Before the coal industry was nationalised in 1946, landowners charged mine owners for the privilege of working their land, a payment known as a 'royalty'. Similarly, the Church Commissioners extracted a royalty from mine owners per ton of coal, in return for the right to cross their land with the coal wagons. Perhaps The Royalty commemorates the point at which the value of the coal being moved was assessed and royalties paid. Of course the area is also notable for the Royalty Theatre. The inaugural General Meeting of the Sunderland Drama Club was held on 2 October 1925 at Meng's Restaurant in Fawcett Street. All early plays were performed in the Victoria Hall and premises were then purchased in Tavistock Place, which was converted into the 'Little Theatre'. On 16 April 1941, the Little Theatre and the Victoria Hall were destroyed, and The Royalty Hall was used for various productions throughout the rest of the war; it was negotiated on a lease from 2 May 1946. On the right today is modern self-catering student accommodation.

LOOKING WEST ALONG CHESTER ROAD TOWARDS GRINDON

COUNCIL MINUTES IN 1930 record a decision to realign Chester Road between the 'top gates' of Bishopwearmouth Cemetery and the Grindon Mill. This was to be broadened and called, naturally, the Broadway. The section of road to the north would be kept and renamed – you guessed it – the Narrow Way, although it was later changed to Nookside. The streets built in the 1930s leading from the Broadway were named on a schematic basis beginning with either 'W' or 'B'. It is likely that Grindon was originally 'Green Dene'. On early nineteenth-century maps the area is dominated by the North and South Grindon farms and Grindon Mill Farm, with Grindon Lane running north from Durham Road to Grindon Mill, then on to South Hylton. Of course it has all been built on now, but there are still three streets whose names commemorate the

three farms. Penshaw Monument stands out very clearly (as it does throughout much of County Durham) and the prominent Hastings Hill on the left with its Iron-Age remains is also obvious.

THIS AREA IS now covered by housing. The land beyond the Grindon Mill Inn was purchased by Sunderland Corporation in the 1950s from the Lambton Estate, Vaux and others, and the big council housing estates of Pennywell (Clowes Croft Farm) and Hastings Hill were built there. The post-war Sunderland Corporation's massive housing estate developments, such as Pennywell, Grindon, Red House, Hylton Castle, Thorney Close and Town End Farm, have all passed into the ownership of Sunderland Housing Group, public–private partnership. Since the housing stock transfer in 2000, there have been huge improvements to the quality of social housing in the city and the formerly notorious council tower blocks at Gilley Law, Hendon and the East End have been transformed. In the spirit of the post-war town planners, Sunderland is now building more new social housing than any other local authority in the UK.

THE ENTRANCE TO THE ROYAL INFIRMARY

SUNDERLAND'S FIRST PURPOSE-BUILT hospital was the Ignatius
Bonomi-designed Sunderland Infirmary at the foot of Chester Lane
(later Chester Road). The hospital had an operating theatre and
sixty beds, and had been built from private subscriptions on land
given by Lord Londonderry in 1822. Multiple murderess Mary Ann
Cotton, who poisoned at least ten victims, worked at the hospital as
a nurse. With the opening in 1867 of Potts' Gothic-designed Royal
Infirmary under the Presidency of Sir Hedworth Williamson, the
Chester Lane hospital became redundant and subsequently functioned
as a theological college for the Methodist Church. After the college
relocated, the building became consecutively a Methodist place
of worship (until the 1901 opening of Cleveland Road Primitive
Methodist Church), a school for St Mary's Roman Catholic Church,
and is presently occupied by Sunderland University. The Royal
Infirmary stood in New Durham Road, where it moved in 1867 from
the earlier building in Chester Road. The original central building was
designed by Joseph Potts and several extensions were added by John

Eltringham between 1882 and 1911. Nursing staff were provided between 1873 and 1888 by the Tottenham Sisters, who were a Protestant version of the Roman Catholic Sisters of Mercy.

THE INFIRMARY WAS granted the title 'Royal' by King George V in 1911. The Accident and Emergency Unit is just beyond the car. It is thought that William Milburn may have designed the porch of the Royal Infirmary with its wise owls gazing down on passers-by, because they usually featured in his hospital designs. Milburn claimed that it was because they were the 'patrons of constipation'! In fact, owls are usually associated with medicine and with wisdom with this link dating back at least as far as Ancient Greece, where Athens, noted for art and scholarship, and Athena, Athens' patron goddess and the goddess of wisdom, had the owl as a symbol. The site of the old Royal Infirmary is now covered by the Royal Courts apartment blocks, which are named after members of the Royal Family.

ETTRICK GROVE FROM THE NORTH

THE PLACE NAME of Barnes was first recorded in 1351. By the seventeenth century it had been divided into High Barnes and Low Barnes. High Barnes passed from the Bowes family to William Ettrick in 1673. Ettrick was originally from Dorset, but arrived in Sunderland in 1661 to take up the post of Collector of the Port. After 1845, the High Barnes Hall was demolished and rebuilt as a new 'Home for the Aged' which still stands on the site today, with a date stone indicating 6 August 1900 as the start of its construction. The building was run by the Little Sisters of the Poor from its opening. Meanwhile, the Low Barnes house and estate passed eventually to Richard Pemberton Esq., who was from a notable local family with extensive land-owning and industrial interests. Richard Pemberton made it the principle family seat until the nineteenth century, but the encroaching urban sprawl of Sunderland led them to relocate to Hawthorn Tower on the Durham coast to the south. Following the departure of the Pemberton family the property appears to have been let to a laundry company.

THERE WAS A long twenty-year campaign to have a park established there. In 1904, the land was bought from a Mr Punshon by Colonel Thomas Reed, a member of the Sunderland family which had a very successful printing and publishing firm, and the chairman of the parks committee. He paid £8,500 for the land and the park was laid out by 2,798 unemployed men supervised by skilled gardeners. Along with the bowling greens, other principal features were added to the park; a lake with islands, timber bridges and an open bandstand were constructed in the valley floor. The valley bottom and bank sides were laid out as a pleasant walk, with rolling lawns and trees in shrub planting. The steeply sloping grass banks around the bandstand formed a south-facing 'amphitheatre'. Very recently the ceremonial gold key used to open the park was bought by a Whitburn lady at a Christies' auction. The park was opened on 6 August 1909 and the key was presented to Colonel Reed. The park became quite dilapidated in the later twentieth century, but has now been restored to its former glory with Lottery funding.

SOUTHWICK VILLAGE CENTRE FROM THE WEST

'SOUTHWICK, ORIGINALLY CALLED Suddick, is now (...) a village of no mean proportion. Its population numbers about 10,000 souls and it is beautifully situated on the North bank of the Wear about 2 miles from Sunderland.' (Luke Crown, former shipwright, speaking of Southwick in the 1840s). The Green was reshaped in 1912 to represent the outline of a ship and from this angle you can see the shops of old Southwick on the south side of the Green. In the 1940s and '50s they included Finkles' cake shop in the centre, to its left was Miss Tonks' off-license and to the right of Finkles was a general dealer. Further down towards South Terrace was Annie Fell's fruiterer's shop and Cook's paper shop, with the old Savoy Cinema over on the left. The Sunderland Corporation clock was one of a number dotted around the town, which lit up In the darkness and fed off the mains electricity. The post office is where the

Rowntrees' sign is and beyond that, hidden from view, is the Smith's Arms. The cobbles are very prominent in this picture – paviors used big double-handled 'poss sticks' to get them even.

THIS PICTURE (LEFT) was taken from the former Southwick Co-op at the top of Stoney Lane. Next to it was the Tramcar Inn. The tramcar is a surprisingly smooth and quiet mover, and potentially quite lethal. The first accident involving electric tramcars was during the opening procession, when the No. 2 (operated by the vice-chairman of the Tramways Committee) ran into the back of the No. 1 (operated by the chairman!). Electric trams were better protected than horse trams regarding accidents involving pedestrians, because they had lifeguard shields which could be lowered, however, accidents will happen. Apart from people being run over, others died when trying to steal rides on the step or hanging on to the back. Apparently, Southwick boys were particularly good at this specialised form of surfing. It was also quite fashionable to injure yourself when trying to mount or dismount from a tram before it had stopped moving, plus there was the added obstacle of long and trailing dresses. In fairness, it must be pointed out that trams were remarkably safe vehicles and the number of accidents very small in relation to the miles covered and number of passengers carried.

SOUTH HYLTON
RIVERSIDE FROM
THE NORTH EAST

LOOKING ALONG THE Wear from the eminence of Southwick, the shipwright and
shipbuilder Luke Crown wrote in his old age that 'looking west the view that is spread
before you is one of the most charming and lovely aspects. The scenery of this delightful
Panorama is composed of Hill and dale, Rock and crag, Tree and shrub, Castle and Cottage,
River and burn, In fact everything that has a tendency to beautify a landscape is there.'

This vision of rural arcadia is taken from North Hylton, near the Shipwrights Arms at the point where the Hylton Ferry crossed. Ferry and steps are visible and Penshaw Monument is visible on the horizon. Until 1796, the ferries at South Hylton served the main route between Sunderland and Newcastle. The chain-operated ferry was used for vehicles and the rowing boat for passengers, the latter continued in use until 1957. The ferry was a favourite subject for the artist Ralph Hedley. In the background is the Shipwrights Arms which, together with the Golden Lion, served not only the ferry trade but also the keelmen who journeyed up and down the river.

THE SHIPWRIGHTS ARMS stands in Ferryboat Lane, a name which reflects its significance as a major river-crossing point. The public house claims to be haunted and, if one is not driving, a couple of drinks might produce the desired illusion. This area was once very heavily industrialised and to the left, off the picture, was Dawson's Pottery. There was also a foundry and other industrial premises. At one time, smaller ships were built here and even further upstream at Cox Green, so what is now a pleasant rural scene was once a thriving industrial environment. In 1854, there were at least half a dozen shipyards in the area (including the original Bartrams). However, long before that this inn and the Golden Lion on the opposite bank were part of the chain of inns serving the needs of thirsty keelmen. The Shipwrights was one of nine pubs which were condemned by magistrates in 1928 for operating a system of women's 'boxes' – box clubs were a method of saving small amounts of money each week then having a pay-out at the end of the year. The Licensing Sessions claimed that this encouraged women to frequent public houses and the practice was dropped here the following year.

If you enjoyed this book, you may also be interested in …

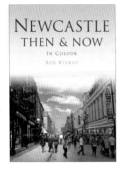

Newcastle Then & Now

ROB KIRKUP

The city of Newcastle has a rich heritage, which is uniquely reflected in this delightful, full-colour compilation. Contrasting a selection of forty-five archive images alongside modern photographs taken from the same location, this new book reveals the changing faces, buildings and streets of Newcastle during the last century.

978 0 7524 6566 1

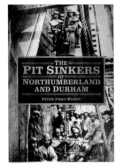

The Pit Sinkers of Northumberland and Durham

PETER FORD MASON

Newcastle and the collieries along the Tyne had a long tradition in coal mining, for which the centuries-old method of shaft sinking was a must, whether it was for shallow bell pits or deep shafts. In the north-east the mining community was strong and here shaft sinkers were considered the 'elite of miners'. With previously unpublished photographs, this book is a must for all those interested in the region's industrial heritage.

978 0 7524 8094 /

Haunted Wearside

DARREN W. RITSON

From eyewitness accounts of unexplained sightings to the search for evidence of ghosts, this book features over fifty chilling tales of ghostly encounters from around Wearside. Featuring the ghostly nuns of Franklin Street, a headless horseman in Newcastle Road, and the phantoms who haunt the Royal Infirmary, *Haunted Wearside* is guaranteed to make your blood run cold. Richly illustrated and drawing on historical and contemporary sources, this collection will delight everyone interested in the paranormal.

978 0 7524 6088 8

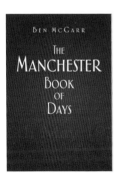

The Manchester Book of Days

BEN MCGARR

Ideal for dipping into, this addictive little book will keep you entertained and informed. Taking you through the year day by day, *The Manchester Book of Days* contains quirky, eccentric, shocking, amusing and important events and facts from different periods in the history of the city.

978 0 7524 8308 5

Visit our website and discover thousands of other History Press books.

www.thehistorypress.co.uk